this book belongs to

....

....

Life is really simply but we insist on making it complicated. Confucius

Life is not a problem to be solved, but a reality to be experienced. Sored Kierkegaard

I have found that you love life, life will love you back. Arthur Rubinstein

Life is ten percent what happens to you and ninety percent how you respond to it. Lou Holtz

Succes is not final, failure is not fatal: it is the courage to continue that counts. Winston Churchill

What you get by achieving your goals is not as important as what you become by achieving your goals. Zig Ziglar

Life is like riding a bicycle. To keep your balance you must keep moving. Albert Einstein

If I cannot do great things, I can do small things in a great way - Martin Luther King Jr.

You don't always need a plan. Sometimes you just need to breathe, trust, let go and see what happens. Mandy Hale

Some people look for a beautiful place. Others make a place beautiful. Hazmat Inayat Khan

Happiness is not by chance but by choice. Jim Rohn

You are never to old to set another another goal or to dream a new dream.

Never love anyone who treats you like you are
ordinary. Oscar Wilde

Luck is what happens when preparation meets opportunity. Seneca

You do not find the happy life. You make it.
Camilla Eyring Kimball

You must do the things you think you cannot do.
Eleanor Roosvelt

It isn't where you come from. It's where you are going that counts. Ella Fitzgerald

Believe you can and you are half way there.
Theodore Roosevelt

If a man knows not to which port he sails, no wind
is favorable. Seneca

Hang on to your youthful enthusiasms – you will be able to use them better when you're older. Seneca

Time heals what reason cannot - Seneca

We suffer more often in imagination then in reality.

Seneca

There is no charm equal to tenderness of heart.
Jane Austin

Being deeply loved by someone give you strength
while loving someone deeply gives you courage.
Lao Tzu

Don't wait. The time will never be just right.
Napoleon Hill

Love yourself first and everything falls into line.
Lucille Ball

Difficulties strengthen the mind, as labor does the body. Seneca

At night, you have to believe in the light.

Dwell on the beauty of life. Watch the stars, and see yourself running with them. Marcus Aurelius

Magic is believing in yourself, if you can do that,
you can make anything happen. Goethe

Jump, and you will find out how to unfold your
wings as you fall. Ray Bradbury

Sit with warriors. The conversation is different.

Being positive in a negative situation is not naive.
It's leadership.

Kind words are like honey.

You are your sanctuary.

Your direction is more important than your speed.

Happiness, like running, is a skill that can be practiced. Start by thinking happy thoughts for 10 to 15 minutes a day.

Once you've matured, you realize silence is more powerful than proving a point.

Gratitude is not only the greatest of virtues, but the parent of all the others. Cicero

Succes consists of going from failure to failure without loss of enthusiasm. Winston Churchill

Courage doesn't always roar. Sometimes courage is the little voice at the end of the day that says:'I will try tomorrow.' Mary Anne Radmacher

Dreaming, after all, is a form of planning. Gloria Steimen

If you can dream it, you can do it. Walt Disney

Life shrinks and expands in proportion to one's
courage. Anais Nin

The future belongs to those who believe in the
beauty of their dreams. Eleanor Roosvelt

The most common way people give up their power
is by thinking they don't have any. Alice Walker

By being yourself you put something wonderful in the world that was not there before. Elliot

Keep life simple!

CPSIA information can be obtained
at www.ICGtesting.com
Printed in the USA
BVHW062224090621
609011BV00005B/883

9 781471 756597